How do
clouds form?

Lynn Peppas

Author
Lynn Peppas

Publishing plan research and development
Sean Charlebois, Reagan Miller
Crabtree Publishing Company

Editorial director
Kathy Middleton

Editor
Reagan Miller

Proofreader
Crystal Sikkens

Photo research
Allison Napier, Samara Parent

Design
Samara Parent

Production coordinator
Samara Parent

Prepress technician
Katherine Berti

Print coordinator
Katherine Berti

Illustrations
Katherine Berti: page 8

Photographs
Dreamstime: page 5 (right)
Thinkstock: pages 16 (bottom), 17, 18
Other images by Shutterstock

Library and Archives Canada Cataloguing in Publication

Peppas, Lynn
          How do clouds form? / Lynn Peppas.

(Clouds close-up)
Includes index.
Issued also in electronic format.
ISBN 978-0-7787-4475-7 (bound).--ISBN 978-0-7787-4480-1 (pbk.)

          1. Clouds--Juvenile literature. 2. Weather--Juvenile literature.
I. Title. II. Series: Peppas, Lynn. Clouds close-up.

QC921.35.P47 2012   j551.57'6   C2012-901510-5

Library of Congress Cataloging-in-Publication Data

CIP available at Library of Congress

Crabtree Publishing Company

www.crabtreebooks.com   1-800-387-7650

Printed in Canada/042012/KR20120316

Published in Canada
Crabtree Publishing
616 Welland Ave.
St. Catharines, Ontario
L2M 5V6

Published in the United States
Crabtree Publishing
PMB 59051
350 Fifth Avenue, 59th Floor
New York, New York 10118

Published in the United Kingdom
Crabtree Publishing
Maritime House
Basin Road North, Hove
BN41 1WR

Published in Australia
Crabtree Publishing
3 Charles Street
Coburg North
VIC 3058

Contents

Cloud watching

Have you ever watched clouds as they move across the sky? Are the clouds thick or thin? Are they white or gray? Clouds are made up of tiny water **droplets** or **ice crystals**. Each droplet is so small and light that it floats in the air.

Will you need an umbrella? Or is it a day for shades? Look to the clouds for the answer.

Clouds are clues!

Clouds come in many different sizes, shapes, and colors. Different kinds of clouds bring different kinds of **weather**. Clouds are like clues. Learning about clouds can help us know what kind of weather to expect.

5

Earth's water cycle

Earth's water moves from oceans, to air, to clouds, to land, and back to oceans.

The **water cycle** is the movement of water from the earth into the sky and then back down to the earth again. Clouds are an important part of this cycle. Read on to learn more about the different parts of Earth's water cycle.

From liquid to gas

The Sun heats water from oceans and lakes. When water is heated it changes from a liquid into a gas called **water vapor**. Water vapor is warm air that holds tiny water droplets that cannot be seen. Water's change from a liquid to a gas is called **evaporation**.

From gas to liquid

Water vapor rises into the sky. The air high up is colder than on the ground. As water vapor rises, it cools. As it cools, the water vapor starts to **condense**. This means the vapor changes into tiny water droplets.

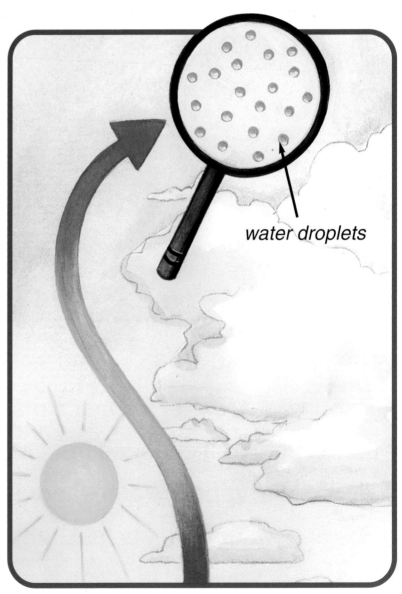

water droplets

A cloud grows larger as more water droplets or ice crystals join together.

A cloud is created!

The water droplets form around tiny pieces of dust in the air. Millions of these droplets join together to form a cloud. If the **temperature** in the cloud is very cold, the water vapor freezes to form ice crystals.

Precipitation

The water droplets in a cloud join together and get larger and heavier. When water droplets become too heavy to stay in the air, they fall to the ground as **precipitation**. Precipitation is any form of water that falls from clouds. Rain, snow, and **hail** are kinds of precipitation.

Snowfall

Ice crystals are tiny pieces of ice. As the crystals fall from the clouds, they join with other crystals to form snowflakes. In winter, the air near the ground is often cold enough to keep the snowflakes from melting.

ice crystal —

All about clouds

*Clouds are like containers that carry Earth's water. **Wind** moves clouds across the sky. Clouds carry water from one place to another.*

You can learn a lot about clouds just by looking at them. For example, clouds look dark when they are filled with water droplets. The water droplets block the sunlight from shining through the clouds. If clouds are dark and look heavy, rain or snow is on its way!

cirrus clouds

cumulus clouds

stratus clouds

Naming clouds

In 1802, a man named Luke Howard gave **Latin** names to different kinds of clouds. The names describe the cloud's shape. We still use Howard's cloud names today. The main kinds of clouds are **cirrus**, **cumulus**, and **stratus**.

Cirrus clouds

In Latin, the word cirrus means "curl." Cirrus clouds look like thin, flowing curls or waves. Cirrus clouds form high up in the sky. These clouds are made up of ice crystals because the air high up is very cold.

14

Cirrus clouds are also called "mares' tails." A mare is a female horse. Do you think these clouds look like a horse's tail?

Weather patterns

When you see cirrus clouds it usually means the weather is sunny. Cirrus clouds are also a sign that the weather will change within the next day.

15

Cumulus clouds

Cumulus clouds are puffy and white.
In Latin, the word cumulus means
"heap" or "pile." Cumulus clouds look
like piles of cotton balls floating in the sky.

cotton balls

16

When cumulus clouds grow taller and darker they are called cumulonimbus clouds.

Weather patterns

Small cumulus clouds are a sign of good weather. Sometimes cumulus clouds grow upward quickly. Then they are called cumulonimbus clouds. These are tall, dark gray clouds. They bring heavy rain, thunderstorms, snowstorms, or hailstorms.

Stratus clouds

In Latin, the word stratus means "layer." Stratus clouds form low to the ground in layers, like sheets. They can cover the whole sky like a gray blanket. Sometimes these clouds block the Sun's light.

Fog can make it hard for people to see where they are driving.

Weather patterns

If stratus clouds sink lower to the ground it means there will be light rain or snow. Fog is a stratus cloud that forms on the ground.

Contrail clouds

Not all clouds are formed by Earth's water cycle. Contrails are clouds made by airplanes flying high up in the sky. The term contrails is a combination of two words: condensation and trails.

An airplane's engine releases water vapor as it flies. The water vapor freezes and forms ice crystals in the high, cold air. This creates a contrail cloud.

How to make your own rain

You will need a parent, teacher, or caregiver to help with this experiment.

Materials:

water

kettle

ice cubes

metal baking sheet

What to do:

1. Put water inside the kettle and have an adult heat the water until it boils.

2. Do you see steam coming from the spout of the kettle? This is evaporation. The heated water has turned to water vapor in the air.

3. Place ice cubes on the metal baking sheet. This will make the sheet cold. Have an adult hold the metal sheet with oven gloves over the steam from the kettle. You will see water droplets form on the bottom of the baking sheet. This is condensation. Condensation happens when the hot water vapor cools quickly after hitting the cool baking sheet.

The water droplets will grow bigger and eventually fall from the sheet. You will then have created your own raindrops!

Words to know

cirrus Thin, high-forming clouds made of ice crystals
condense To change from a gas to a liquid
cumulus Puffy, white clouds
droplet A tiny drop of water
evaporation The change from a liquid to a gas
hail Frozen balls of ice that fall from clouds
ice crystal A small piece of ice that floats in the air in cold weather
Latin An old language that was used thousands of years ago
precipitation Rain, snow, or hail that falls from clouds to the earth
stratus Thick, gray, low-forming clouds
temperature A degree of heat or cold
water cycle Describes how water moves between Earth's surface and the sky
water vapor Water that has changed from a liquid to a gas
weather What the air is like at a certain time and place
wind Naturally moving air

Index

Learning more

Books:
What is Climate? by Bobbie Kalman. Crabtree Publishing, 2012.
The Water Cycle by Bobbie Kalman and Rebecca Sjonger. Crabtree Publishing, 2006.
The Weather by Deborah Chancellor. Crabtree Publishing, 2010.

Websites:
http://eo.ucar.edu/webweather/cloudhome.html
www.weatherwizkids.com
www.northcanton.sparcc.org/~elem/interactivities/clouds/cloudsread.html